decorating

with

white

decorating
with
white

Jeanine Larmoth
And the Editors of
Victoria Magazine

Hearst Books
A Division of Sterling Publishing Co., Inc. • New York

Copyright © 1996 by Hearst Communications, Inc.
All rights reserved.
This book was previously published under the title
Victoria At Home with White.

Produced by Smallwood & Stewart Inc., New York City
Edited by Laurie Orseck
Designed by Susi Oberhelman

Library of Congress Cataloging-in-Publication Data
Available upon request.

10 9 8 7 6 5 4 3 2 1

Published by Hearst Books,
A Division of Sterling Publishing Co., Inc.
387 Park Avenue South, New York, N.Y. 10016

Victoria and Hearst Books are trademarks owned by
Hearst Magazines Property, Inc., in USA,
and Hearst Communications, Inc., in Canada.

www.victoriamag.com

Distributed in Canada by Sterling Publishing
℅ Canadian Manda Group, One Atlantic Avenue, Suite 105
Toronto, Ontario, Canada M6K 3E7
Distributed in Australia by Capricorn Link (Australia) Pty. Ltd.
P.O. Box 704, Windsor, NSW 2756 Australia

Manufactured in China

ISBN 1-58816-191-9

Contents

Foreword

Do I love white? Why else would I have raised a young lad in a living room decorated primarily in white? Before you jump to conclusions about my lack of good sense, let me assure you that is was wise indeed. All the furniture was slipcovered in washable fabrics—and in an afternoon the room could look as fresh as spring daisies. A spill was not a terrible tragedy, it was an excuse to make my things sparkle. Curtains were whitework, table coverings damask, so you see that I was not without variety in my passion for white.

When my son went off to college, I added other colors, and he was amused at what seemed my "doing things backward." I think that what I had learned living with white was my primer for decorating. Many of us begin with a clean palette. As our confidence grows, we become more adventuresome, but we never outgrow our reverence for what white can do for us. In an instant disparate objects are united, in a moment elegance is achieved. We can have summer with the toss of a cloth, or winter with the warmest whites.

I hope that you enjoy *Decorating with White,* and that you find ideas for every room in your home. White, so perfect as nature's paintbrush—just consider an egg or a seashell—is welcome everywhere.

NANCY LINDEMEYER
Founding Editor, *Victoria* Magazine

Introduction

White is the purest color, and, as we are taught in childhood, no color at all. Rather, white throws off every color of the rainbow, rejecting each with elegant indifference ~ wiping away "moonlight like mud," to borrow poet Wallace Stevens' words. But what the physicists teach of the nature of white matters little. For most of us, whether we are buying clothes or decorating our home, white is a color, and a favorite color at that.

The reasons for decorating with white are as various as those who use it. White is capable of endless subtleties; ever fresh, ever responsive, it is the only color that can fill the whole house with beauty without becoming irritating, strident, or tiresome. It also unifies as no other color can, smoothing rough corners, slipping past small faults, encircling disparate objects in a single, very personal composition.

White is also a measure of extremes, allowing no compromises, demanding perfection. It can be solemn and lighthearted, serene and frivolous. In architecture, white is the elegance of Regency London, with its rows of cream-colored houses trimmed in white; the sobriety of tall-spired clapboard churches in New England; the grace of Southern colonial mansions on rolling lawns; the whimsy of gingerbread orna-mentation on Victorian cottages; the proud triumphal arch; and the sensuously lacy Moorish screen. White has washed over the humblest adobe dwellings and the grandest palaces.

From antiquity, white has expressed a society's loftiest aspirations, the need for dignity and the yearning to breathe, if only for a moment, a higher air. At the same time, whether aloof or intimate, the poetry of white helps each of us give expression to our most private voice.

A Color of Many Moods

One of the many qualities of white is its ability to change from surface to surface. Here, the molded planes of a Victorian mantelpiece, a shining china vase, and sprigs of lily of the valley become a study in whites, enriched by the tinted fashion prints on the wall.

It may be the most ethereal of hues, but it is neither reticent nor shy. White is positive, assertive, and highly visible. Over the centuries, its power has been understood and exploited. Ever sage, Queen Elizabeth I, when visiting her courtiers, stepped from boat or coach clothed in radiant, silver-threaded white so she would stand apart from her attendants and the welcoming throng. The American poet Emily Dickinson drew attention all her life for wearing only pristine white dresses, whose spareness matched her verse. Military leaders such as Joan of Arc, George Washington, and Napoleon rode white horses so that they could be recognized from a distance, reassuringly present, even on the turbulent battlefield.

In decorating, white is capable of creating almost any style or mood. It can be traditional, modern, rustic, or romantic, depending on the shades used, the shapes chosen, the textures combined. It is splendid at the seaside or at the top of a skyscraper. It can make an

A traditional decor is opened up, and a large room becomes even larger, with white walls, furniture, and appointments. Creamy upholstery rather than dark heightens the illusion of openness and space. Unruly flowers and the gaiety of a glittering crystal chandelier enhance the room's friendly and receptive air.

17

interior as bold as the bleached white dwellings in our visions of antiquity in the glaring sun of Greece and Egypt. It can be as stark as the primitive adobe houses of the American Southwest, or as simple as a whitewashed Alpine retreat by Le Corbusier.

White can make a room as refined as a palm-shadowed, wicker-filled Edwardian conservatory, redolent with the perfume of sultry flowers and moist earth, where the sound of violins drifts through the open doors of the adjoining ballroom. Tufted settees and side chairs lose their heaviness when covered with white-on-white satin stripes, lose their stiffness when dressed with white linen.

Even the most traditional furnishings become dramatic statements when white is used to emphasize their classic shapes. Comfortable club chairs, boxy sofas, Sheraton- and Regency-style furniture, down-filled banquettes and love seats ~ all are renewed and refreshed with upholstery of white linen, linen blends, heavy cotton, or patterned damasks, lifting and brightening entire rooms. To

White weaves an old-fashioned, country spell in this kitchen. Pale stripes on the wall, a pale checkerboard floor, glossy coats of paint on worn chairs and tables, and the decorative touches of straw hats and old china are an irresistibly sunny combination.

A kitchen cupboard, mellowed by time and use, becomes a showcase for shades of white. The cabinet's coat of ivory paint is contrasted by the sharper white of lace-edged napkins. Gray and silver pitchers, clear glasses, light green bottles and a tiny clutch of pale ranunculus add to the calmness of this rustic vignette.

soften the whiteness requires no more than the plumping of a few pillows covered in faded tapestry or Irish-knit wool in a sofa's corner, the draping of a mohair throw in misty plaid or a tasseled piece of antique brocade over the arm of a chair.

With equal ease, white can evoke the streamlined, Art Deco world of the twenties and thirties, when it cast off its innocent airs and became hard, shiny, even decadent. In that sophisticated era, white was everywhere: fox furs; clinging, bias-cut crepe de chine dresses; calla lilies leaning in frosted glass vases on white grand pianos; quilted white satin bedcovers.

In those days, designers utilized white for the home with exceptional skill. No two personalities better illustrate the enormous difference in effects that can be achieved with white than the English decorator Syrie Maugham and the French master Jean-Michel Frank. Maugham was famous for painting even priceless antiques white. "I seem to see [the figures of the mid-twenties] dressed in white, in

Faded café au lait wall-
paper, just a tone away
from antique white, serves
as a congenial foil for
postcards in sepia.
Spring bulbs, picking
up and magnifying a hint
of red in the cards,
introduce an unexpected
touch of color.

A wall whitewashed
over layers of paint repeats
the tones on a weathered
old lantern, now chipped
by time. Straw hats
echo the harmonies of
creamy yellow, gray, and
white. A bowl massed
with pink peonies provides
the sole contrast.

frosty immobility against a white screen," writer Beverley Nichols has said. "Why white? Because that was the period's distinctive hue. And the person who was most responsible for this fashion, which later became a craze, was Syrie Maugham . . . she had delicious taste. But though she had a most delicate sense of colour, her greatest triumphs . . . were won in pure white. She performed miracles with whites and off-whites, and creams and ivories, and the palest oyster-greys. . . .

"Her own house, at 117 King's Road, Chelsea, was as pretty as a narcissus in the snow, as pretty as a silver feather on a pane of winter glass. . . . Were I painting an impressionist picture of the great room on the ground floor, which was at the centre of the house, and indeed, its raison d'être, I would begin with an immense screen that stood in the far corner. It was fashioned from hundreds of strips of mirror, and always in front of it there were great bunches of white flowers ~ madonna lilies, peonies with their tousled heads, lilacs as thick as cream, foxgloves, looking strangely sophisticated in this

In this tropical setting, swags of white fabric looped from the ceiling suggest a tester over a four-poster bed, opposite; the lace on the bed linens and tables seems to cool the room with a soft breeze. A white latticework screen stands ready to shield a doorway, above left. The final grace note: a sprig of bouvardia laid by the pillows, above right.

White has an endless capacity for changing the mood and style of a setting. Used on a traditional sofa, it makes the familiar, comfortably curved lines seem new. The white woolen throw adds still another layer of tone and texture.

unusual setting. The flowers seemed to dance in recurrent rhythms as one moved round the room."

In contrast to Syrie Maugham's effulgence, Jean-Michel Frank preferred white for its austerity. His geometrically pure furniture was devoid of superfluities, his interiors free of excess. The designer achieved a wholly modern look by emphasizing the subtle shadings and variations in surface textures. His tables were covered in glossy white lacquers or pebbled gray sharkskin, his small chests and screens in straw marquetry, his walls in vellum or pale shantung.

As the work of both these designers illustrates, not only are there infinite numbers of whites, there are innumerable other shades that we experience as white. Among these are the naturals ~ pale stone, light or weathered woods, faux bamboo, the silvery green of eucalyptus leaves, the silky gray of pussy willows; old gold, silver, pewter; mirrors, crystal, and glass. There are neutrals to be included as well ~ such hues as khaki, wheat, mustard, putty, taupe. Sometimes even faded prints and monochromatic patterns ~ stripes on stripes, for example ~ can appear as white in the right setting.

WHEN WE DECORATE A HOUSE, a room, or a garden with white and its extended circle of neutrals, we focus not on the bold or the obvious but on nuances, differences in tone, gentle gradations, subtleties of shade, and quiet harmonies. We savor contrasts of shape and silhouette, light and shadow, surface variations that are barely discernible, allusions that would be lost in another color.

White is an invitation for us to extend our imagination, to reconsider outworn rules, to capture the delicate, to perpetuate the illusive, to step into privacy and calm, a world of our own invention.

Pure whiteness may not be possible, and it is not always desirable. In this boudoir, satiny peach stripes on a creamy white settee enrich the soft, cosseting glow and peaceful intimacy of a private corner.

Classical Details

The buildings of ancient Greece and Rome are still the standards by which our own architecture is judged. From their triumphs came our knowledge of balance and proportion, lessons in light and shadow, appreciation of structure and harmony, yearning for dignity and the loftier plane. Also from the ancient world came the supporting motifs and details that eighteenth-century architects in particular transformed into white plasterwork arabesques: miraculous columns; acanthus tendrils and honeysuckle vines, rosettes, cherubs and cupids, and light-footed goddesses, and endless, endless swags. Among the several exceptional English architects of the period, perhaps the best known is Robert Adam. After careful study of Roman ruins, Adam adapted the decorative elements from the wall friezes and terra-cotta vases he

Architectural white, a dominant force since the Golden Age of Greece in the fifth century B.C., lives on in the classical details of turn-of-the-century mantelpieces and a newel post at the foot of a staircase.

saw for the homes of his patrons. With singular grace, he combined filigrees of white plasterwork with classical columns, bringing a sense of surging movement and joyful lightness to even the most formal interior. Though he often used icy white touches to set off pure colors on walls and ceilings, Adam also used them in combination with other whites, near whites, creams, palest tints, and stone grays. We recall these classical details when we frame a ceiling or paneled walls with white moldings, set a classical head or figurine of plaster on a rococo bracket, pick out a mantelpiece or pilaster in white paint, put a potted plant on a white column stand, or set a column-based lamp on a desk. These architectural motifs, even in the tiniest spaces, continue to lend, as they have for centuries, an atmosphere of elegance and serenity, together with a lightness of heart.

An Evolving Canvas

I have always had white in my life," says former fashion model Mary Baltz, whose comfortable cedar-shingle house on eastern Long Island stands as a testament to this passion. The least limiting, most freeing of colors, white is a sheer delight in her life because it lets her do many of the things she enjoys most: creating the vignettes, the small arrangements, that vary from day to day, almost from hour to hour, throughout the house, on the porch, and in the garden.

White also encourages Mary in another pastime: painting and repainting walls. "If I have a color other than white on my brush," she says, "the process has stopped for me once I put it on the wall. With white, the canvas is never finished. White lets me expand what my mind can do, see how I can rearrange, do things differently ~ what I would do with that piece at Christmas, what I would do with it in summer." Thirty to fifty gallons of paint ~ creams, ivories, vanillas, bisques ~ always await her next project, whether it is redoing her bedroom walls or twenty-four chairs for a party that same evening.

Matching doesn't matter. "With white, you don't have to think about what goes or doesn't go," Mary points out. The gracefully curving sofa in her living room, for example, is layered with white

In the Baltz house near the sea, light plays over layers of different textures and shades of white, over the trays of shells and lavish bunches of roses it is Mary Baltz's joy to arrange. To increase the coziness of the sofa, heaps of soft down-filled pillows replace the back cushions.

linens of different shades and different ages, as well as a white mohair throw. A long slip that peeps from under the beige linen duster that she wears is edged with a cherished old piece of lace of her mother's, as well as five other kinds she has found at antique shops.

Everywhere in the Baltz household, along with the mix of tints and textures, the new and the old, there is a melding of the valuable and the less so. A yard sale chair bought for three dollars shares the space with Mary's grandmother's silver tea service, a treasured memory from her childhood; Limoges china from her husband's family is joined by odd plates and saucers found in thrift shops or given to her by friends. Nothing is saved just for special occasions. "If we don't use the good things," Mary explains, "they become antiques in our time."

Though the house glows with the windswept freshness of white, and an atmosphere like a dream, there is nothing dreamlike about it. White is the easiest color to live with, according to Mary, because it is the easiest color to clean. Should a tumble in the washing machine fail to restore a piece, Mary applies bleach, peroxide, and baking soda, separately or in combination, until it is pristine and sparkling once more. As a result, there are no sacred objects in this home, and nothing is off-limits. Unrestrained, the family's white-pawed dog, Marley, jumps up on the sofa to look outside; Mary's three-year-old daughter, Abigail, jumps up beside him.

Every afternoon, a mood of calm descends on the house. Music from her husband Laurence's tape collection fills the rooms. Candles are lit beside bunches of roses, a fire may crackle in the entry fireplace, and Mary can nestle down among the white, embroidered linen pillows piled on the sofa. "It's nice sometimes to feel like a queen," she says. "The white things all around me ~ the silver, the roses, make me feel that way. Sunlight with white, candlelight with white, light changing, light beaming off silver and crystal ~ it's all part of using everything you have each day."

Precious crystal and silver appear on tables throughout the living room, ready to catch the shifting light year round. Having several tables in one room means more places for Mary to create beautiful vignettes.

Above left, a rose motif unifies a collection of mismatched
pieces of china in an old wooden hutch near the
kitchen. Above right, a cotton skirt for the washstand
and white shutters turn an unattractive
bathroom into a special spot. Opposite, floral prints fill
the walls in a corner of the living room.
Mary found the bird cage and the needlepoint fish
pillow at a local antiques shop.

Fine Points of Fabric

To decorate a house or a room with white means that we exchange a range of colors for a palette of subtleties, a spectrum of refinements. The "absence" of color in white not only makes us focus on variations in tone, it increases our awareness of differences in texture ~ rough and smooth, substantial and fragile, shiny and matte ~ on the light and shadow that play over a surface. We notice the sheen of glossy objects, the chalkiness of whitewashed walls, the filminess of curtains forming pools on the floor that make a room, though still, seem breeze-filled. Even in homes dominated by color, white is often preferred for bed, bath, and table linens. The quality of such linens and the care they have received can make them one of a family's most precious heirlooms, a source of pride, to be passed down from one generation to the next. The fortunate bride has in her trousseau fine old pieces ~ some, perhaps, showing the handiwork of a grandmother or an aunt: cambric handkerchiefs, linen sheets, crochet-edged

pillowcases and tea towels, lace tablecloths and doilies, knitted shawls. If the use for which they were originally created has gone out of fashion, there are a thousand new purposes to be invented for them. The embroidered tea towel can be laid over a curtain rod or become a cover for an occasional table or a tray; the lace tablecloth turns into a field of snow when it is laid on a bedspread.

  The purity of white fabrics has always set them apart for special purposes; the finest of them have provided some of the most highly valued luxuries of this world.

"TO LOVE BEAUTIFUL LINEN," wrote French novelist Louise de Vilmorin, "is to love fair weather, fair weather . . . that one can acquire and carry home. Solemn and joyous, dear to the heart and unrivaled in our lives, linen crosses the centuries signifying elegance, tradition, and

An old-fashioned huck linen towel with a hand-crocheted edging becomes the covering for an occasional table at teatime, opposite. The lamp is daintily skirted in sheer cotton with scalloping along the top and bottom. Above, antique lace tablecloths can be swagged over a window or fall richly in the hangings of a bed, so that each tender fold can be appreciated.

serenity. By its changelessness, its vitality, linen renews, every day, the ties between modern life and that of other times. . . ."

Flax, the blue-flowered plant from which linen fiber comes, was grown in Iraq and Egypt as early as the sixth century B.C., and there is evidence that linen was woven in Neolithic times in what is now Switzerland. At first, the fibers were spun into thread by women using only their fingers. When the distaff and spindle were developed to replace this method, they became symbols of womanhood; in ancient Greece, the goddess Athena, who was credited with the invention of spinning, was often shown holding a distaff as a symbol of peace.

It was not until about A.D. 1520 that the spinning wheel made the distaff and spindle obsolete, and it was still the only way to spin linen thread when America was settled. In the colonial period, linen played almost as vital, if less explosive, a part as tea in the Revolution: Making their own linen was just one more way for colonists to prove their economic independence from England. Spinning and weaving were taught by local weavers, many of them immigrants from Scotland and Ireland. The weavers encouraged their young pupils by offering a prize of enough linen for a new dress to the girl who spun the greatest amount of thread in a given time. In Boston, classes in spinning and weaving were held in the State House in winter and on the Common in summer. The well-known diarist Judge Samuel Sewall described a spinning bee on Boston Common in which "five hundred fashionable women took part," and compared spinning's role in the American home with that in ancient Greece.

Dowries often included a spinning wheel, and the bride was expected to have in her trousseau sheets she had made from thread she

Works from yesterday's skillful fingers become treasures for today. On an eighteenth-century tester bed, a hand-knit cotton counterpane ebbs and flows with interlocking ribs, opposite and above. Instructions for intricate patterns such as these were offered in "Godey's Ladies' Book and Magazine" in the nineteenth century.

*Cotton eyelet, above left,
fresh and unsophisticated, is
a favorite for bedrooms.
Above right, openwork
embroidery shows the tiniest
hint of pink. Opposite, a
stack of summer linens
includes a Jacquard-weave
throw, a matelassé bed-
spread, a diamond-pattern
cotton blanket, and a sweater-
textured cotton blanket.*

herself had spun. A decade before the Revolution, spinning bees were held by the Daughters of Liberty, eighteen young ladies who spun flax from sunup to sundown to avoid buying British cloth. At Mount Vernon, Martha Washington herself supervised the making of a linen and wool cloth, called linsey-woolsey, for colonial army uniforms.

The best flax has always come from temperate countries with large supplies of fresh, soft water, so essential to linen production. Because flax fibers are brittle, spinning and weaving were done in a warm, moist atmosphere, and the finished cloth was laid on the grass to bleach under blankets of dew, sun, and moonlight. The French sent their linen cloth to Holland to be bleached, because it was thought that Dutch meadows gave it a unique radiance.

Though chemical bleaches have now replaced the old bleaching greens, the results are still evaluated, as they were then, in terms of the fabric's exact degree of whiteness; some of the categories are "pure white," "half-white," "quarter-white," and "cream."

Types of linen are defined by the fineness or heaviness of the thread used and the looseness or density of the weave. At one end of the scale is the coarse canvas once used for sails, elegant Irish sheets so opulent and inviting on a bed, and the supple damask that reflects candlelight on a well-dressed dinner table. At the other end of the scale are the gossamer linens such as batiste, a fine, tightly woven fabric developed in the thirteenth century by a weaver named Baptiste of Cambrai, and the even sheerer, more transparent lawn, named for the French town of Laon, where it was first woven at the beginning of the sixteenth century. (Today, these fabrics are sometimes made of other fibers; cotton batiste and cotton lawn are two examples.)

At the beginning of the nineteenth century, damask, one of the most popular and prized weaves used in the home, was still being made by hand, but it was also being produced by Jacquard looms. These intricate and costly looms employed cards with holes punched in them to control which threads were raised over the shuttle and which

Windows show off the sheerest delights. Opposite, the summer sun is muted by a drape of white-on-white, awning-striped voile pulled back with a satin bow. Above, the essence of romance, an antique lace curtain patterned with roses and medallions seems to promise views of a garden.

47

remained flat. The more elaborate the damask pattern, the greater the number of cards used. The result of what has been called a "hide-and-seek with light" is a matte design on a satiny ground. Though it is reversible, the "right side" of damask is the one with the satiny ground. Traditionally, the patterns were meant to complement the designs of prestigious furniture, silver, and china, such as Sheraton, Wedgwood, and Spode, and often drew on Louis XVI, Empire, Queen Anne, fifteenth-century Italian, and Elizabethan motifs.

Traditional summer dress for a Southern mansion, straw matting replaces heavy woolen rugs; shapely muslin slipcovers protect chairs from the too bold sun; breeze-light netting is whisked around the chandelier; and lace films the tall windows.

THE FRENCH HAVE A SAYING that someone is "raised in cotton," meaning that he or she is wonderfully spoiled. The Roman poet Lucretius compared the fiber to white clouds.

Cotton was cultivated in India before 2000 B.C. In the eighth century A.D., the Moorish conquerors of Spain brought with them cloth woven from cotton grown in Persia, India, and China. It was the Crusades, however, that made Europeans cotton-conscious. After the last Crusade, which ended in 1291, merchants established headquarters in Venice, where they continued to deal with Saracen traders for cotton goods. By the end of the sixteenth century, cotton-linen weaves were being produced in French cities such as Lyons and Rouen. A stronger, all-cotton fabric called cretonne was developed in the French village of Creton at about the same time.

The opening of sea trade with the East in the seventeenth century made cotton available to rich and poor alike. Among other treasures crammed in the holds of the returning ships of the Dutch, English, and French East India companies were printed and painted cottons from India. These inexpensive cottons, later called chintz, quickly became a craze, and the threat that they posed to the powerful English weavers caused the government to prohibit their importation.

This only stimulated imitation, and English textile printers soon were making a chintz that was a better match for English taste.

Cotton's final ascent to popularity came after the invention of the cotton gin by Eli Whitney in 1793. Traveling through America, the French writer and politician Chateaubriand thought the cotton plants he saw in the fields resembled "white roses."

The quality of cotton, like that of linen, derives from a combination of the length of the fibers (those of Egyptian cotton, which is considered the best, are about seventeen inches long), the fineness of the yarn, and the number of threads per square millimeter. Because they are usually lightweight, cottons are trimmed with only a hint of lace, a bit of cutwork or openwork such as eyelet, or flounces to underscore their airiness. One of the sheerest cottons is muslin, a great favorite of the ladies of the Napoleonic era in the eighteenth

A quilted cotton pillow, opposite, extends an invitation to dream an afternoon away. Above, a pleasing medley of fabrics freshens and warms a bedroom: blue gingham and rickrack-edged pillows; an old and fragile lace doily, now a touch of whimsy swept over a settee; a matelassé bedspread and pillow covers.

Whorls like seashells make a cotton matelassé twin bedspread
a welcome guest at the table, above left, while
a crisp, subtly textured towel tries a new role as a dresser
scarf, above right. Opposite, a whitewashed
portable tea table serves in the garden at the height of
summer. In winter, it becomes an occasional
table with a hemstitched linen cloth edged in cotton lace.

century. Today, two of the sheerest types are voile, a muslin with a plain, open weave, and organdy, a transparent muslin that takes on a permanent crispness when it is bleached.

THE SINGULAR BEAUTY of lace makes it one of civilization's most artistic achievements. Though forms of lace existed in ancient Egypt, and probably even earlier, the creations that wove spells of enchantment around royalty were first made only 450 years ago. Needlepoint lace was invented in Venice toward the end of the sixteenth century. According to a local legend, lace was created by the sweetheart of a sailor who had been taken prisoner by Barbary pirates. Patiently awaiting his release, she reproduced with her needle a piece of coral that he had brought her earlier from his travels. The net she created became her bridal veil, and the origin of Venetian lace.

One of the most genial things about the tea table is its mobility. It can happily be set up wherever the sun is softest or a fire glows in the fireplace. Here, in a living room corner, it is swathed for a summer afternoon in a tailored sheer linen cloth with white-on-white embroidery.

The first needlepoint lace was called *punto in aria*, or "stitch in air." Though a single needle, using primarily buttonhole stitches, worked on a mesh anchored to parchment on which the design was drawn, the parchment was removed once the lace was finished. At first the patterns were as geometrical as those already used in reticella, a form of cutwork embroidery. Gradually, however, needlepoint lace freed itself from its geometric constraints and captured instead fantasies of flowers intertwined with leaves, garlanding, musical instruments, cupids, nymphs, and mermaids.

Even a humble kitchen table and chairs take on a holiday air with the addition of a lace cloth, opposite. The vintage machine-made fabric is the color of fading hydrangeas. Above, a pitcher of lemonade and a weathered white tray for cookies, cake, and little sandwiches become more evocative sheltered by a doily and a cage of net.

Bobbin lace, which originated in Flanders in the seventeenth century, was more closely related to weaving. Threads wound on bobbins were twisted and braided around and between pins stuck in a parchment usually supported by a pillow.

The craze for lace was such that in about 1719 the English were spending some two million pounds sterling on Flemish, French, and Italian imports. Governments, roused by so much money going abroad, prohibited lace's importation, and many countries started their own lace-making industry. Exquisite laces were produced by women in convents; queens and their ladies-in-waiting also put their fingers to work, much as they had once embroidered tapestries. In the eighteenth century those who could afford lace wore it from head to toe and lavished it on their beds and dressing tables until even mirrors and toiletries were veiled in the precious fabric. The preferred type was the superbly white and delicate French Valenciennes. When personal bathing returned to fashion in about 1750, Alençon and point d'Angleterre, also from France, were used to adorn bath shirts and line wooden tubs.

The invention of a machine for making *fond de Bruxelles*, the net used as a base for making lace, in Nottingham, England, in 1768, created a fashion for machine-made lace for clothing. Eventually, Jacquard looms were modified to produce bobbin lace, and in 1880 the invention of a machine called the Schiffli made it possible to reproduce needlepoint lace as well. By the early nineteenth century, lace-making had virtually disappeared as a craft, except in a few workshops specializing in luxury goods. Today, although lace is not produced on the scale it once was, it is still being made by hand, and machine-made lace for the home can be readily found through mail-order houses.

At a cottage on Long Island, dove gray and
white striped cotton chintz and white linen slipcovers
hide winter's more sober fabric. A tablecloth
patterned with squares dresses a table set for afternoon
refreshments, above left, and airy white linen
curtains wave in place of heavy draperies, above right.
Opposite, lace frosts a teatime table, and a
festive white bow dresses up a delicate oval mirror.

A Passion for the Past

I have a passion for things made with the hands ~ lace, embroidery, petit point, tapestry, everything," says bridal couturiere Pat Kerr. Her strong feeling for handwork is something that she connects with her childhood on the family farm in the Deep South. All around her were women patiently and happily laboring over the intricacies of embroidery, crochet, and quilting. In the 1960s, while traveling with her husband, an international financier, Pat began to gather ceremonial robes and fans in Japan. "I've gone rummaging everywhere," she recalls, "through the darkest alleys and into the most imposing castles. I've gone from Paris to the south of France, from Marrakesh to Shanghai. Looking at a piece, I can remember exactly when it came into my life." The textiles and costumes she finds are not stuffed away in drawers and forgotten. "I

Bridal treasures in Pat Kerr's collection, clockwise from top left: lace handkerchiefs that once belonged to Queen Victoria; a turn-of-the-century dress webbed in lace and encrusted with embroidery and pearls; a pair of courtly satin slippers; and a nineteenth-century painted silk satin fan.

live daily with the pieces in my collection," she says. "My houses are filled with things like hand-loomed French draperies and hand-loomed Napoleonic sheets. I am grateful to those who took care of them in the past."

In London, where she lived for eighteen years, Pat immersed herself in the study of lace and began acquiring the pieces that have made hers one of the largest and finest collections in the world. Among her treasures are gossamer pieces from the sixteenth century, pieces made by and for Queen Victoria, and innumerable examples of personal favorites such as Belgian Duchesse and English Honiton. In her eyes, lace is the epitome of luxury, representing a sense of time that will never come again. "Lace reminds me of a more civil way of life," she says. "There's something very connecting globally about it. Like music, it's all the same language."

Lace for Everyone

A house without lace is like a house without music. Even in the most chaste modern home, there is always a corner that might be lovelier with a cobweb of lace spun over it. It might be little more than a shade for the last lamp to be turned out at night or lace-edged napkins for the tea table. It could be a wispy streamer to tie around the crown of a summer hat that ornaments the back of a chair; eyelet edging for the shelves of a dresser or an armoire; a lace tablecloth that turns a picnic in the park or dinner served beneath the trees into a celebration.

While the sight of women skillfully plying bobbins or needles has grown rare, the art of making lace by hand has been almost lost, and even finding machine-made lace of a hundred years ago has become difficult, it is still possible to gather together all the lace that one needs. Fortunately, small mail-order companies make it easy to receive lace through the post. Many such companies are as near as calling the local telephone information number, which will in turn transfer the call to the Toll-Free Directory.

Through companies like London Lace, Rue de France, Linen and Lace, Heritage Lace, and J. R. Burrows and Company, lace lives on. There are ready-made pieces: pillow shams, curtains of all lengths,

The morning sun is muted by medallions of lace, above, appliquéd on a window shade. Opposite, a bathroom shelf with a lace runner becomes a setting for flowers and photographs. A simple cotton doily creates a charming shield for a lampshade.

Best wishes for a "gute Nacht" are framed with a tiny frill of eyelet on a boudoir pillow sham, above left. A swag of scalloped lace is prettily drawn back from a lace panel with a satin bow, above right. All these elements come together in an utterly feminine bedroom, opposite.

tablecloths, lace doilies or handkerchiefs to line a basket holding sweet, fresh-baked bread or rolls; place mats for the tray that serves Sunday morning breakfast in bed.

Mail-order companies also provide lace by the yard and lace panels that can be cut up for a hundred different uses. All that is required is inventiveness, a pair of scissors, and the ability to make hard choices about which frothy piece should go where: Should a curtain of Nottingham lace flutter at the window, as it might have at the Brontës' home high on the Yorkshire moors? Would a cherub-patterned piece be right as a runner on a dressing table, as a swag over an antique bed, or as a valance?

What rose catalogs are to rose lovers, lace catalogs are to lace lovers: a way to dream away winter evenings. As you glance through the catalogs and garner ideas, visions of a summer cottage, wildflowers in a jar in front of a small, lace-hung window, may dance through your head. On the other hand, it may not be possible to wait that long.

Summer's Delight

The easy elegance of summer finds expression in an old wicker chair, its paint worn away gracefully by the years, its cushions covered in once-popular cretonne cotton fabric. A simple hat with a wide brim and crushed organdy crown, absentmindedly left on the chair, lends a casualness that is the essence of a summer setting.

Every season has its moments of white, moments when it is the dominant color and dictates the mood. Nothing, for example, fills the air more than the blue-shadowed snows of winter, the light in a room that is, as the poet Wallace Stevens saw, "more like a snowy air, / Reflecting snow. A newly fallen snow / At the end of winter when afternoons return." The snowy air, frost-feathered windows on a winter's morning, the mirror of ice on a pond that will be etched by skaters' blades are all aspects of white.

Spring and autumn, too, have their hours reserved for white. In spring, petals like dainty shells scatter over the ground. If the fragile scented air and soft breezes had a color, it would surely be white. And in autumn, white mists drift in veils over country roads, cloak the stars in ermine, envelop the stroller by the ocean. The season's whiteness is the giant moon that turns cornfields to silver, the first frosts that make each blade of grass a piece of crystal.

66

Furniture arrayed in
linen damask and draped
with fringed shawls
reflects the summer world
outside. Everything in the
room is pale, from the
candles on the table and
the roses to the antique rug.
The few pieces of dark
furniture serve to sharpen
the effect by contrast.

Despite the strength of these claims, however, summer is the true season of white, radiant and commanding as the sun's blaze, soft and honeyed as the perfume of jasmine or nicotiana blooming in the night. Summer's whites are as varied as fields of tossing daisies; delicately nodding Queen Anne's lace; tiny sparks of fireflies; billowing clouds at the seashore.

White is, above all, the color of our dreams of summer: endless beaches, whitecaps tossing like the manes of galloping horses as far as the eye can see, umbrellas lining the sand, gulls wheeling in the sky, seashells discovered on a barefoot stroll. White symbolizes bright hope and fullness, and freedom from care.

It is for all these reasons that we decorate our summer homes with white. And when we wish to re-create this sense of anticipated pleasure in our our homes for the summer months, or indeed to capture it in our homes all year long, we borrow ideas and objects from the summer settings we have known and loved, or read of or imagined.

Everything says summer, opposite: the love seat slipcovered in white canvas, an etched-glass hurricane lamp, and a treasure box encrusted with shells. Below, an album of sepia photographs is bordered with captions in calligraphy, and, for a bookmark, a creamy satin brocade ribbon.

In the Old South, carpets were rolled up and replaced with sisal mats every summer, lace curtains substituted for draperies, unused fireplaces turned into backdrops for flowers. Today it may mean shielding windows with old linen shades, bamboo blinds, louvered shutters, or a drift of lace, or leaving them uncurtained save for a single swath of voile caught up in a rosette to one side.

Re-creating the patterns of summer places may also mean painting furniture white or choosing pieces paled by time, pieces that look as if they were found in a cobwebbed attic: an old steamer trunk to be used as a coffee table, a weathered ladder to hold plants or books. A rocking chair with a rush seat, a garden bench, a wire-back ice cream parlor chair become welcoming places to sit.

Upholstered pieces might be dressed at their summer best in slipcovers. Easy to remove and wash, slipcovers allow us to be a little more languorous, more relaxed and carefree. Faded, large-flowered, cotton cretonne on overstuffed chairs and sofas promises

In a hilltop cottage high above Los Angeles, costume designer Theadora Van Runkle uses white as a backdrop for warm-colored paisley and flowery chintz, opposite. The white oak table with a faux-marble top and an antique marble statue, above, keep white actively at play in the room.

comfort and ease. Cool and elegant linen echoes the luxurious days when F. Scott Fitzgerald's Gatsby strolled across the lawns of his estate. White canvas, often used on boats or in cottages by the sea, gives a room a tidily shipshape appearance. A gauzy web of voile drawn over an inexpensive chair transports it to a time when mosquito netting covered everything in the South during summer, from the chandeliers and gilded frames of paintings to the four-poster beds.

Floors can also become summery when they are glossily painted, antiqued, or bleached and glazed with white; when they take shelter under worn, flower-patterned vintage rugs, inexpensive old Oriental carpets, or always endearing rag rugs. They are equally summery left bare and polished, the wood's grain their only ornament.

A Victorian chair, above, upholstered in white gives a room the look of a turn-of-the-century holiday resort. Opposite, past summers are also recalled by white wicker side chairs and a chandelier with glass shades. To allow the room maximum light and air, the curtain is no more than a giant pouf of twill with a floor-length streamer.

EVEN THE KITCHEN can step back to summers past: Imagine wooden cabinets, stripped of paint or distressed; shining white china displayed on the open shelves of a Welsh dresser; an antique coffee mill, china or painted metal canisters on counters, a china pitcher and basin that might have stood on the dresser in a resort hotel in days gone by. Old, still usable utensils might be hung conveniently on the walls. A picnic basket can serve as storage space for table linens and silver, or the white candles that are always there in case of an electrical storm. A sunny windowsill becomes a year-round garden with a row of silvery-leafed herbs or potted white cyclamen. Battered hats, caught in the rain more than once, wait on pegs by the door.

Once the basics of a room are established, other summer signatures placed here and there will add to this reverie of summer's ease: dried bouquets of baby's breath in putty-colored stoneware jars; collections of seashells heaped in silver-rimmed Mexican glass boxes; white-branched coral and hurricane lamps on small tables; sepia

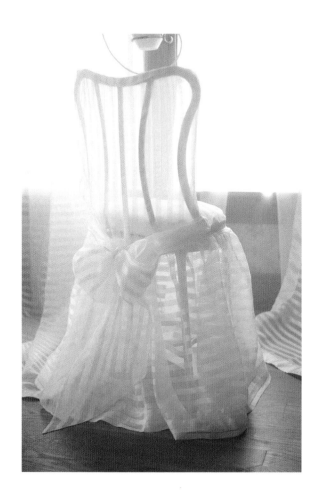

The simplest wrought-iron chair is transformed into
a vision of summer when painted white and
given a sheer, bowed skirt, above left. The tie-back of
the curtain is just one more place to tuck a
blossom, above right. A graceful way to divide space
is with a curtain dramatically drawn back
and left to pool on a bare, polished floor, opposite.

A china pitcher and bowl,
once the means to morning
ablutions, play a decorative
role in a summery guest
room, right. The corner of a
porch turns into a bedroom
with an old metal bed and a
chest converted to night table
by a bunch of flowers and
a wispy fall of lace, opposite.

photographs in twig frames on the wall; Ball jars of beach glass in pale blues and greens, catching the light; butterfly collections or pressed ferns under glass; model sailboats setting out to sea on the mantel.

With such evocative touches all around, home becomes a setting of never-ending summer, a place of refreshment and repose, outside of time where life is always young, where a breeze seems to be stirring, even when everything is absolutely still.

A metal garden chair,
brought inside and
softened with a brocade
and lace boudoir pillow,
gives a room a welcome,
sunny feel even on
the darkest winter days.

*Washing up at the kitchen
sink is a more pleasurable
task with an antiqued
wood counter, an enamel
plate for soap, a haze of
airy curtains, and a vase
of Queen Anne's lace.*

Even when there is no
mosquito nearer than
a hundred miles, it is still
a delight to sleep under
netting hung over the
bed. In place of a window
shade, a panel of lace
elaborates the theme, and
the romance, of the netting.

83

Perfection in White

Some things are inseparable from the white that consitutes their color. White is part of what they are; no matter what other colors they may sometimes be, when they are white they seem to take hold of our imagination, to become greater, and, often, to become symbols. The white horse, running free, is the essence of motion, more spirit than animal, a mystical ghost of itself. The white cat sitting with its front paws close together is, for the moment, all that is modest. The white swan floating on a pond, long neck arched and ruffled wings folded, is synonymous with serenity. The white dove flying skyward carries our hopes for peace.

The expressiveness of white speaks of the soothing and the flawless, of the otherworldly and of worldly perfection. White creatures and objects alike seem caught, like angels in their radiance, between heaven and earth; real, but not entirely

A blithe bouquet of perfection for summer, clockwise from top left: straw spun round with a dulcet veil; a clutch of double-petaled narcissus; wedding finery for a ring bearer and flower girl; crocheted gloves and a lace-edged handkerchief.

so. Some of the most perfect whites ~ a pleasure to behold, a pleasure just to think about ~ are, of course, flowers: the snowdrop, first and bravest bud of mid-winter; the icy-petaled narcissus with its crystal scent; lily of the valley bells; the calla lily, exotic as the white tiger, no matter where it grows; the fragile camellia, whose concentric petals might have been drawn by a compass. Even entirely earthly things become extraterrestrial when they are white: white peaches; white marble; romantically billowing nightdresses; the faultless pearl; a lady's fresh white gloves, a gentleman's white tie and tails; the riches of Devonshire cream spooned over scones and strawberry jam; white birches; new-fallen snow; satin wedding slippers; white parasols; white mushrooms.

"If you have two loaves of bread," says an old adage, "sell one and buy lilies." A moment of perfection is yours.

A Palette of Seashells

A house near the sea carries its own special obligations. The interior must reflect the light from the expansive sky, the fleeting clouds that forecast the day's occupations, and the distant roar of the ocean that is a constant reminder of the shore with its glistening, tufted grasses, undulating sand, and thousands of tinted seashells scattered there.

Design publicist Susan Becher's cedar-shingle house on eastern Long Island is just such a place. An idiosyncratic Victorian sprawl, full of nooks and crannies, it is a short walk from the beach. The Becher children's numerous activities permitting, that walk is a part of the family's regular weekend program. Because of the location of the house and the rooms' features, Susan decided to fill the house with vintage furnishings rather than with the modern pieces she chose for her city apartment. Shopping locally, she bought worn pine chests and cupboards at antiques stores, whatever pleased her at yard sales, and several pieces of bedroom furniture from a friend who was selling the contents of her home. To this eclectic but mellow mix she added the odd piece discovered on the streets of New York City.

When the Bechers first moved in to their summer house, Susan was tempted to paint the interiors all white. Instead, she chose

soft tones, pale as seashells, to accentuate the Victorian house's splendid architectural details. Some walls are white warmed with yellow, some white blushing with pink, some white cooled with gray. The wainscoting, ceilings, and moldings are a brilliant white, except in the dining room, where diagonal blue and white stripes dance below the ceiling and a mellifluous rosy color circles the bull's-eye ornamentation at doors and windows. This pleasing palette adds to the open feeling of the house, whose old sash windows and enclosed porches barely keep the outside out.

"I think I chose white because it makes the house airier," Susan says. "I wanted a sense of a summer house, though we use it all year round. I've gone for furniture that has simplicity and put slipcovers on it to be easy." Intensifying the summer mood are floors rubbed with white paint and sealed with polyurethane, sisal rugs, lace curtains at the windows, and pale blue and white striped slipcovers. Antique linen and lace tablecloths dress small occasional tables; mounds of white embroidered pillows dress the beds. Here and there white pottery pitchers, a few, giant starfish ~ and of course seashells ~ provide the finishing touches.

The delicacy of the color combinations throughout the house is proof of Susan's great love of color. Not vivid, robust color, but the gentlest shades, the tones of paintings by a favorite artist, Giorgio Morandi: muted sand tones, only a degree from white. Her home stands in constant testament to the joys of her colorful obsession.

In the master bathroom, above, the original Victorian features have been preserved. The bold black and white checkerboard floor provides a dramatic counterpoint to the white walls. The master bedroom, enveloped in a soothing taupe gray hue, opposite, is dominated by a nineteenth-century polished iron bed.

The Bechers' dining room celebrates a sense of light often found in Scandinavian homes. Bentwood chairs circle a harvest table drizzled with lace. The walls, mottled an apricot yellow, are bordered with hand-painted diagonal stripes of blue and white near the ceiling. The floors, rubbed with white paint and glazed, fairly sparkle.

On Intimate Terms

A sweet dream's worth of baby pillows tied up in ribbons and scented with flowers is an extravagant means to turn a bed into a private kingdom. When we are propped amid pillows, even mundane chores ~ paying bills or phoning for appointments ~ are touched with a dusting of glamour.

Almost more than anywhere else, the rooms where we lead the most intimate side of our lives should be a kingdom of white. The same sense of repose that white brings to other areas in the house is even more valuable where we lie down to rest and awaken refreshed in the morning. Everything in the bedroom should suggest privacy and silence; a nacreous shell for the sleeper to curl within. Everything in the room must be an elaboration of the simple pleasure of going to bed.

So, too, is white essential in the dressing room, where we pause to slip on slight, silken things, and in the bathroom, where we submerge ourselves in pure, sensuous pleasure. Both rooms serve as places to prepare for the world outside our personal one, and to reenter it.

Whatever the style of the house, such sanctuaries can continue the theme. In a Cape Cod or saltbox cottage, in a rambling farm-house, this may mean something modest, even severe ~ white eyelet curtains, the chenille bedspreads once a part of every summer lodge, a

Hung in a row from softly padded hangers,
nightdresses, crocheted bedjackets, and peignoirs ~
all things white and frothy ~ become works
of art, opposite. Linens, too, when neatly stacked,
bow-tied, and laid on a lace-edged shelf,
are transformed into decorative objects, above.

Shaker dresser, an old-fashioned marble-topped washstand, a wood-framed mirror, the minimalism with which an Emily Dickinson would feel at home. In an up-to-the-minute modern apartment, it would mean clean-edged, tailored white-on-white stripes, polished white walls and floors, block-letter monograms, a balance of form and proportion.

A romantically out-of-date decor makes its point with a canopied four-poster bed or a crocheted tester, complete with flounces and frills and a mile-high downy duvet, and a dressing-table mirror draped with muslin or lace. The dressing table itself becomes the backdrop for a phalanx of silver-topped scent bottles filled with "white" fragrances whose notes derive from fragile spring flowers.

In the bedroom, if nowhere else, all the stops may be pulled out, the senses thoroughly indulged, fantasies encouraged to do the decorating. To heighten the pervasive sense of romance, windows might be draped, rather than covered, with a vintage tablecloth or looped with lace curtains. A plain lampshade from a thrift shop or

In a bedroom, opposite, a simple chair becomes a table, and a straw hat, mounded with flowers and nestled in tissue, contributes as much to the atmosphere of the room as the flutter of curtains at the window and embroidered handkerchiefs, fragile as butterflies, above.

Palomino-pale wood and mounds of lacy white pillows keep a huge Victorian bed from overwhelming a tiny room under the rafters, above. Opposite, an antique white-enameled bedstead touched with gold is heaped with a queen's ransom of pillows covered in embroidered linen, a wool and angora blanket, and a cotton challis throw.

five-and-dime becomes more evocative trimmed with lace or hidden by a generous handkerchief. A French Provincial or Victorian chair, upholstered in white, can be softened with pillows, some trimmed with ribbons and lace, others flawlessly plain.

The bedroom may gain another dimension from freshly laundered and ironed nightdresses, camisoles, and delicate blouses hung along a wall rather than being incarcerated (and crushed) in a closet. The crisp curves and soft folds, catching light and shadow, make them works of art to see, to feel, to touch.

Elsewhere, more lingerie and bed linens, tied with ribbons and folded on the shelves of a cupboard, become a study in contrasting white textures. On top of an armoire, picnic hampers, small straw suitcases, or wallpapered hatboxes increase the storage space as they add atmosphere to the room. The space may provide, instead, a resting place for dried hydrangeas, roses, and faded larkspur; vintage hats; or, borrowing from Elizabeth Barrett Browning, a group of poets' busts.

Two striking ways to
bring the atmosphere of the
past to the present-day
bedroom: a crocheted tester,
typical of colonial times,
curved over a four-poster
bed, and a gauzy net, once
as characteristic of the
South as Spanish moss.

At the heart of this universe of dreams is the bed itself. In a small room under the eaves, the bed cozily occupies most of the area. Even in a large space ~ French doors opening to the breezes from the terrace ~ the bed becomes a room in itself. Whatever the bed's scope, whether narrow and disciplined as a tented Napoleonic camp bed or like a galleon arrayed in snowy counterpane, swags of netting, and lace curtains, it should dominate the entire room.

A profusion of pillows is always luscious. It can turn the bed into a setting for the luxury of breakfast in bed, taken from a tray covered with linen, croissants kept warm beneath a silver dome, a miniature porcelain coffeepot, a single pale rose in a crystal salt cellar or a bunch of violets in a silver stirrup cup. Pillows make the bed a place from which to order one's world, as English ladies often did in the past. In *The Rainbow Comes and Goes*, Lady Diana Cooper describes her beautiful mother in frilled silk nightdress under a cream flannel kimono-shaped robe, her head wrapped in a knitted vest, its

Identical iron bedsteads, opposite, become as different as the sleepers who rest in them by the choice of bed linens. The bed on the left has the tailored simplicity of cream-on-white stripes; the bed on the right, covered in a Marseilles spread, cascades with lace-encased pillows.

sleeves wound under her chin like a medieval coif, making her pillows the center of the world. "I see her sitting cross-legged . . . writing endless letters with a flowing quill pen," Lady Diana writes. "On her knees was balanced a green morocco folding letter case, with blotting paper and a pot of ink which curiously enough, never got splashed on the Irish linen sheets. It had a bristled pen wiper and pockets for letters written and unwritten. Having no telephone, in urgency she would give a stylised scream to attract her maid Tritton, to whom she would hand a letter marked 'Messenger Boy' to be put in the box."

The bathroom, too, should be furnished as seriously as every other room is furnished. Muting the bright glare of porcelain might be weathered wooden cupboards, a subdued Oriental carpet, roses framed under glass, generous stacks of white towels and cloths, a commodious footed bathtub, and a graceful pedestal sink. For morning and evening ablutions, glass shelves may hold pure bottled water to rinse the face or to spray on to refresh it, self-brewed herbal rinses for the hair and skin, to pour into the bath or smooth on after the bath. A little ballroom chair serves as a rack for a cozy bathrobe or a man-tailored dressing gown in luxurious white satin.

IN THESE PRIVATE SANCTUARIES, the strictures of fashion have no sway. We might choose a voluminous cotton nightdress like the one actress Merle Oberon, as Cathy, wore as she was gathered up in Laurence Olivier's arms in *Wuthering Heights*. We might sit at the dressing table to brush our hair in a slither of silk crepe. In the shadows of late afternoon, we might even decide to change into a soft and flowing tea dress before taking tea at a small table there. Comforting extras might include a hot water bottle in a handsome, quilted jacket

There is no more natural place for the cleanness of white than the bathroom. But it becomes romantic when every detail, from lace-edged washcloths and towels to a blossoming branch of a fruit tree, presents different shades and shapes of white.

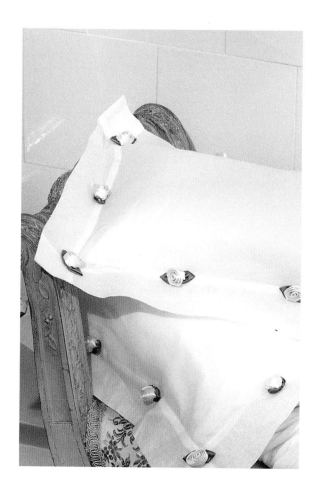

Roses are a beguiling motif to soften the sometimes
hard-edged bathroom, opposite. They may
garland the wallpaper, be stitched on rose-scented
sachets for the cupboards, above left, and
on small, downy pillows, too, above right. As a final,
perfect touch, roses might overflow a vase on an
old-fashioned marble-topped stand.

A vintage bedspread rack has another use as a place for towels to hang, airing and showing off their fringed crochet edging at the same time. The same rack may also serve a secondary purpose, displaying a bunch of white roses as they dry.

to warm the bed on chilly nights while final preparations for sleep are being made. Sachets with herbs ~ lavender, rosemary, chamomile ~ to induce sweet dreams are tucked under the pillows; a nightdress is artfully laid out, as if by a well-trained ladies' maid, when the curtains are drawn against the night.

On a round table beside the bed, layered with old linens and laces or a vintage tea cloth, are nighttime musts, the things we will sleep less well without: a scented candle lit to fill the room with the

The ample china basin ~ resting here on a cutwork linen runner ~ was a commonplace in Victorian homes. Filled to the brim with cool water and a mixture of herbs or with soothing rosewater, it still provides a special way to freshen in the morning.

welcoming aroma of evergreen boughs or ripe peaches; a pile of books (among them, a pretty journal for jotting down the day's thoughts); a dainty clock or heirloom pocket watch; a cherub, swan, or miniature ship in a bottle; a beloved photograph of face or place framed with shells or dried rosebuds; a music box to play a dulcet tune.

With tender and familiar objects all around us, we can retreat and rest, in a mist of white, comfortably and securely, like the fairy-tale princesses we knew so well as children.

Caring for Delicates

eautiful possessions ~ a lace tablecloth, a satin pillow, an heirloom shawl ~ require beautiful care, respect for the hands that may have worked day after day over a few inches. One aspect of caring is patience, for caring requires time and a willingness to take pains. Another is enough space in which to hang or gently fold these treasures without crushing them ~ a cool, dark, dry place that helps prevent fibers from discoloring or deteriorating.

Before a vintage piece is put away, it must be cleaned. Washing is hazardous at best; bleaching or spot cleaning is better avoided; and brushing may break fibers. Preferably, the piece should be laid under a fiberglass screen and vacuumed with a low-powered, hand vacuum cleaner. In a pinch, the nozzle can be covered with net instead and passed over the cloth without touching it.

Stronger fabrics should be taken to a coin-operated dry-cleaning machine, with hooks and

Spacious storage is a must for vintage fabrics, clockwise from top left: an antique silk throw; bed linens tied with ribbons and piled in a basket; a covey of monogrammed pillow shams.

eyes or anything that might catch swathed in net. Frail areas must be patched with net that is lightly stitched in place with a fine needle and silk thread. Before being put in the machine, the piece should be sewn into a loose bag made from a nylon net curtain. Newer, less delicate pieces may be washed after vacuuming. First, they must be soaked in plain distilled water in a nonreactive plastic, glass, or smooth enamel basin. This should be followed by soaking in distilled water and purified natural soap, an anionic detergent, or an anionic detergent combined with liquid non-ionic detergent. After a final rinse in distilled water, the piece should be laid flat on a fiberglass screen to dry.

Before storing, any valuable piece must be wrapped in acid-free paper, extra amounts of it stuffed in the folds. Small, flat pieces such as ribbons should be covered in the paper and rolled, right side out, on cardboard cylinder ~ also wrapped in acid-free paper ~ and stored lying flat.

Best Friends

Even the closet is refreshed with the light touch of blue and white. Two classic patterns ~ paisley leaves and crisp stripes ~ cover a hatbox and a smaller nest for silk flowers, satin bows, or velvet cockades.

As a neutral, white flourishes with any color. Clashes and conflicts are unknown. White is the great harmonizer. Green and white are fresh as nature, red and white cheery as a peppermint stick. Pink and white are the bloom in a spring bouquet. Black and white form the ultimate contrast, a pair of polar opposites, the essence of chic, whether the keys of a grand piano, the marble tiles in the foyer of a castle in Ireland, or Fred Astaire's top hat, white tie, and tails.

Of all combinations, however, blue and white is the most cordial, the most universally loved. It has the clear-edged contrast of black and white without the sometimes overbearing drama. It is serene but not cold, dulcet without being cloying.

Since blue makes white appear whiter, one of blue and white's most appealing characteristics is its look of cleanness ~ a windswept sky in summer, the clear blue sea, sunny-day clouds. Since the sky and sea, in turn, suggest air and water, this most ethereal color combination

In a sunny living room,
pillows sporting pale blue
flowers, stripes, and lattice
patterns, above, along
with a cozy sofa and a blue
and white rug, right, send
out as bright a welcome as
the light flooding through
the windows and the mood
of gentle disarray.

is also the most domestic. And nowhere has the domestic poetry of blue and white been better expressed than in Holland. The superb Dutch genre painters, such as Vermeer and Terborch, invariably used blue in their interiors, whether the subject was a woman pouring water from a jug or reading a letter, a laughing group gathered in a kitchen, or a couple strolling in an enclosed garden. The blue may be the rich crumpling of a satin skirt, a bit of sky glimpsed through a half-open door, the velvet upholstery tacked on a rigidly upright chair, or a pitcher standing on a chest in front of a luminous, whitewashed wall.

So it is appropriate that it was the Dutch who played a major role in spreading one of blue and white's greatest artifacts ~ blue and white china ~ through the Western world. Though Chinese blue and white porcelain was already known in Europe by 1575, when the Florentines attempted an imitation, it was by no means a popular enthusiasm. In the early seventeenth century, however, the tide turned. The ships of the East India companies, with the Dutch taking the

The pleasure of blue and white, whether in bold modern china or dainty and old-fashioned transferware, opposite, is part of what makes a kitchen a magnet for company. Above, a plump Spode pitcher keeps company with simple blue-rimmed cups and saucers.

lead, found a newly appreciative audience for Orientalia, especially Chinese porcelain. By 1660, potteries at Delft, as well as at Nevers in France, were producing notable blue and white faience, or tin-glazed earthenware, whose designs were based on those featured on Chinese and Japanese vessels.

Though at first the Dutch reproduced the patterns, gradually they let their fancies run free, bringing together Oriental elements and their imaginings. Tiles, jugs, bottles, and plates came alive with monsters, dragons, slender ladies, and fat gods. The success of the Delft faience was such that much of the blue and white ware subsequently made was called delftware, regardless of where it originated.

The rage for blue and white china was so pervasive that virtually every country in Europe attempted to produce its own version. In many countries the wealthy set aside entire rooms to display their collections. In 1670, Louis XIV built a garden structure in the Chinese manner, the Trianon des Porcelaines, at Versailles. The exterior

In a white setting, the merest hint of blue ~ a penciling of blue stripes on walls or pillows, for example ~ is like a glimpse of a peerless sky on a day of endless summer. In an instant, even a winter world seems filled with sunshine.

Blue and white patterns set
each other off brilliantly.
The stripes of bed linens, the
diamonds of a quilt, and
tiny flowering embroidery on
pillowcases provide a visual
excitement that makes
the use of any other colors
unnecessary. An offhand
bouquet of delphinium adds
a deeper note of blue.

Legacies of the past, opposite: Gracing an
antique washstand is a nineteenth-century blue and white
transferware pitcher and basin whose patterns
descend from early attempts to capture the elusive secret
of Eastern porcelains. Above, the cool serenity
of a bedroom whose walls are painted a soft blue is an
irresistible invitation to rest.

For the summer cottage, or the city apartment made to feel like one, blue and white fabrics are naturals. Above, blue-on-blue shells border a white cotton towel. Opposite, a hazy pattern of seashells on a pillow sham contrasts with the neat lines of ticking stripes that so often make their home within the sound of the ocean's roar.

was covered with blue and white tiles; inside, panels were painted with blue figures similar to delftware patterns and chairs were upholstered in blue and white striped taffeta. In Sweden, too, a Chinese-style pavilion constructed at Drottningholm by the king housed a gathering of blue and white porcelain, and private homes set aside galleries devoted to the display of the blue and white porcelain they called company china, brought back by the Swedish East India Company.

The lack of real knowledge of the East allowed these countries to create a fairyland of decorative ideas into which they dipped with enthusiasm. Even the new taste for tea drinking played into the craze. By the end of the seventeenth century, the potters of Staffordshire, England, were including blue and white Oriental-style cups and teapots among their wares. The popularity of the quaint patterns later caused English essayist Charles Lamb to write, "I like to see my old friends ~ whom distance cannot diminish ~ figuring up in the air (so they appear to our optics), yet on terra firma still. . . . Here is a young and courtly mandarin, handing tea to a lady from a salver ~ two miles off. See how distance seems to set off respect! And here the same lady, or another ~ for likeness is identity on teacups ~ is stepping into a little fairy boat, moored on the hither side of this calm garden river, with a dainty mincing foot, which in a right angle of incidence . . . must infallibly land her in the midst of a flowery mead ~ a furlong off on the other side of the same strange stream."

What pleased Charles Lamb pleases us equally today, for blue and white china went from craze to adored tradition, a reliable source to lend charm to our cupboards, to set our tea tables sparkling, to make a warm muffin, a dab of butter, or a breakfast egg appear twice as appetizing. Blue and white china, brought to us centuries ago by merchant adventurers, has become one of the greatest of the many notes of color we rely on to bring a sense of eternal freshness, of blowing wind and blue skies, into our homes.

A whimsically carved
Gothic-style chair, painted
an icy blue and softened
by a pale, flower-sprinkled
cushion, waits in a pool of
light and shadow on an open
porch. A bucket of Queen
Anne's lace and chamomile,
freshly gathered on a
walk through a meadow,
hangs from the back.

Collecting Creamware

Perhaps the best known and most disting-uished blue in the world is Wedgwood blue, the color of a stoneware invented by the preeminent English potter Josiah Wedgwood in 1775. This masterly stoneware, which Wedgwood called jasperware, was the result of the artisan's lifelong interest in the materials used by the ancients.

An earlier accomplishment of Wedgwood's, with even more far-reaching consequences, was creamware. Though a cream-colored, lead-glazed ware was produced in Staffordshire, England, possibly as early as 1725, it took Wedgwood's skill and acumen to put it on tables around the world. He changed its darkish hue into a gleaming white with a smidgen of yellow, the color of butter foaming in a wooden churn. Made of the whitest Cornish china clays and china stone, his creamware also offered a strength and refinement previously available

Creamy white china lends a charming air to country cupboards. The purity of the white, with only a hint of warming yellow, allows the eye to focus on subtle plays of light over even the simplest shapes.

only in imported porcelain. As Wedgwood himself described it, it was "a species of earthenware for the table, quite new in its appearance, covered with a rich and brilliant glaze bearing sudden alterations of heat and cold, manu-factured with ease and expedition, and consequently cheap."

One of those who took his point was George III's Queen, Charlotte, who placed an order for a creamware tea service. So taken was she with the results that she gave Wedgwood a royal warrant as "Potter to Her Majesty" and the right to call the china Queen's Ware. Today, the classical table settings continue to draw collectors. So, too, do beguiling creamware occasional pieces ~ strawberry bowls and fruit baskets, teapots and butter tubs, sugar bowls and melon-shaped tureens, platters, and pitchers, some pierced to a lacy openness, others molded in a basketweave, still others festooned with flowers in relief.

Swedish Light

o country has done more to enhance the light than Sweden, and no country has used white more magically to do so. The long, dark winters and summers brief as illusions have created a yearning for all things reminiscent of fine weather: little gazebos beside sparkling lakes; crayfish feasts held out of doors at long, candlelit tables; the twittering of birds on midsummer nights; a longing for rooms where nature in full bloom seems to come in through the windows.

This craving for the joys of sunlight is surely part of the Swedish psyche. But it was never so artfully heeded as during the reign of Gustav III in the late eighteenth century. It was then that pale colors began to fill Swedish homes and become what we recognize as Swedish style. Influenced by the King's taste, the wealthy stuccoed their neoclassical manor houses throughout the countryside with a palette of summer hues: ochers and terra cottas, straw yellows and suave pinks. Interiors were painted in pale tones as well ~ not pastels, but colors that made it seem as if endless snows had whitened even the light. Floors were left uncovered, their wooden planks sometimes polished, sometimes bleached, sometimes rubbed with white to become yet another reflecting surface. Rooms were left almost empty, with few

In Swedish-style interiors, white becomes a substitute for light. In a corner by a window, a country dresser, hanging shelves, and neoclassical chairs are the color of freshly poured cream, opposite. Old blue and white china mirrors every precious ray of sunshine, above.

pieces of furniture to obstruct their airiness. (It was said that in the home of the botanist Carolus Linnaeus, almost everything could be cleaned with caustic soda and a scrubbing brush.) What furniture there was was copied from the rococo, baroque, and neoclassical styles of France and England; in Sweden, however, where craftsmanship was less refined, the simplified shapes and pale colors these elegant styles were given lent them the charmingly disingenuous innocence of Marie Antoinette's milkmaids hurrying about in their silks. White or pale-colored walls, floors, and ceilings often became canvases for ornamentation as well ~ not the elaborate plasterwork, rich tapestries, rugs, and oil paintings of wealthier nations but fanciful imitations of them. Plain plaster walls might be painted white, with icy-blue wainscoting; stenciled; decorated with trompe l'oeil moldings or imitation plasterwork; painted with festoons of dainty flowers, grisaille, chinoiserie; or adorned with deft replicas of tilework, verdure tapestry, even swags of velvet drapery.

Collections of blue and white Chinese porcelain, prized by Swedish families since they were first brought back by the Swedish East India Company in the seventeenth century, were proudly displayed in open and glass-fronted cabinets. Tall blue and white tiled stoves warmed drawing rooms and dining rooms. Blue and white stripes bedecked walls and divans; satin stripes or plaids of blue, yellow, and white were hung like Turkish tents over narrow divan beds.

What was accomplished in Sweden those centuries ago seems admirably suited to our life today. Swedish style makes us revel in bare wooden floors, find charm in spareness, be at ease with furniture so modest that it makes no demands for formality, and, above all, handle color with the delicacy of something precious. Swedish style provides a guide to the infinite pleasures of white, and an enlightened view of always pellucid blue and white.

Signatures of Swedish style, clockwise from top left: rose stenciling on walls and bleached wood floors; blue-on-blue striped cushions tied on the chairs; a tureen in traditional Scandinavian blue and white; stripes of blue and white on the walls and a diaphanous, deeply draped curtain.

The happy throng is almost
visible seated around
the dining room table, the
portrait of an ancestor
presiding. As likely a part
of the celebration as the
blue and white china that
will be set at each place
are the blue and white tiles
on the fireplace surround
and hanging above the
mantel like a painting.

Under the Sun

Clematis, long one of the favorite cottage vines of England, clambers up, offering visitors as happy a greeting as the open door. "Climbers are among the most useful plants in any garden," wrote Vita Sackville-West. "They take up little ground space, and they can be employed for many purposes."

Centuries ago, our ancestors discovered that one of white's many virtues was to reflect light. When light was bounced back to the sun, the world became a cooler place in which to live. Since then, buildings in hot countries and for hot seasons have been white. What began, in part, as a practical measure has stimulated the creation of some of the most beautiful structures in the world, from the glorious Taj Mahal reflected in a silent pool and the once glittering Parthenon on its hill to the tents that sweep over today's garden parties and the market umbrella sheltering fresh fruits on an Italian street.

White used in furnishing an outdoor place creates a sense of both mystery and luxuriousness, a web of enchantment to be spun over special hours. A patio, terrace, porch, or deck becomes more than ever an escape from dailiness, a place set aside for dreaming with casually placed furniture in white or natural wood, white or pale cushions, vine-threaded trellises, and a profusion of white-flowering

A tiny summer house in a backyard, inexpensively constructed of plywood, echoes the architectural style of the main house. The little house becomes everything in summer: an office, a potting shed, a teahouse, a fairy-tale hideaway for guests.

139

plants. This special place becomes so much a part of the setting that it is as natural as the trees. At the same time, it extends the feeling of the interior to the outdoors and makes the house larger. The outdoor space becomes a kind of breezy, lighthearted extra living room, a pavilion without walls, a functional *folie*.

An outdoor place can also be farther afield, entirely separate from the house. It might be a latticed arbor seat overhung with grape-vines or white roses. It might be a little house, such as the traditional Swedish *lusthus*, hardly larger than the dining table in its center. On a small property, such a little house might be no more than a few feet from the main house; on an extensive estate, it might be a matter of a few miles away on the rolling green or by the water's edge. Though similar in shape to a gazebo, the *lusthus* is surrounded by windows and enclosed by walls so it can be used in winter, when snow is on the ground, with as much joy as in summer. The walls are protection from the wind; the windows let in the sunlight that warms it.

The porch serves as an airy, sun-filled extension of the living room, a wall-less sitting room. White wicker chairs and settees plumped with boldly striped cushions, a surfeit of flowers, pots of hydrangeas, and small tables become inducements to hours of pleasant conversation.

An eclectic mix of cast-off furniture, opposite ~ two styles of wicker chair, a wicker washstand turned plant stand, an old cobbler's bench, and a folding wooden chair, together with a bedspread doing duty as an awning ~ makes a porch an outdoor room in a flowery frame. Above, a straw container and a wicker basket serve as summery cachepots.

An outdoor place can be more portable, too, springing up wherever the blossoms are at their best in the garden, the sun most genial, the shade most delightfully dappled. It may be no more permanent than a bench or table carried there, as handy as a white blanket, quilt, or rug left in the closet by the back door. It can be as quickly set up as a hammock strung between two sturdy trees to loll in on the first summery day.

Even the most utilitarian metal or plastic furniture takes on a softer note when shaded by a white umbrella and set amid flower boxes filled with white geraniums or pansies. Much of the available outdoor furniture, however, offers romantic associations of its own: Victorian cast-iron settees, with their curling ivy tendrils, suggest old gardens of the Deep South; folding bistro chairs and little café tables conjure up the boulevards of Paris; white canvas deck chairs bring back the days of the great oceangoing liners; rough-hewn Adirondack furniture speaks of the forest lodges of turn-of-the-century tycoons. A classic teak

*A porch looks as elegant
as the finest restaurant with
a decor that suits the setting,
right. Chintz-cushioned
wicker chairs, a snow-white
linen cloth with crocheted
lace edging, and a flower-
filled milk jug create
an idyllic setting. Above,
an old-fashioned window
blind with cutwork medallion
proves its flexibility
by serving as a handsome
screen against the sun.*

bench, such as the one that Monet installed in his garden at Giverny, turns an outdoor space into an Impressionist painting.

One of the most frequently chosen types of outdoor furniture is wicker. Among its advantages are its light weight, its relative imperviousness to sudden cloudbursts, its modest cost, and its design possibilities, ranging from the constrained to the fantastical. Wicker furniture has been as much a part of the American summer as lemonade and county fairs since the period after the Civil War, when the superlative craftsmanship of American artisans increased its popularity throughout the world.

But in all outdoor settings, planting is the final note, the tie that binds. Tables, chairs, and occasional pieces are woven into a single composition when they are surrounded by small ornamental fruit trees or citrus trees. Other miracle workers are feathery marguerites in planters or tubs; white-flowering vines such as hydrangea, *Clematis montana*, wisteria, jasmine, and passionflowers, trained up wall or

The essence of outdoor white, opposite: a porch open to the ocean air; a rush-seated rocking chair heaped with palest pink and white cushions, its paint nicely weathering. Lace curtains the corner from the sun. A crocheted hammock stretched across the porch, above, instantly creates a summer place.

trellis, looped over the door or a pergola; rounded, standard topiaries of white-flowering geranium, rosemary, plumbago, or bouvardia; sweet woodruff, white violets, silvery lamb's ears and dusty miller, tucked in crevices or around brick paving.

When English writer Vita Sackville-West began to develop the now-famous gardens at Sissinghurst, Kent, in 1930, inevitably she set aside space for a white garden. She looked forward to a time when a visitor might sit on a wooden garden seat, at the end of a flagstone path, her back to a dark yew hedge, and survey the "low sea of grey clumps of foliage, pierced here and there with tall white flowers." To achieve this effect, she would, she thought, put in soft, gray sweeps of southernwood, artemisia, and cotton lavender, and tall, white Regale lilies. The edging would be the lacy Dianthus "Mrs Sinkins," *Stachys lanata*, or rabbit's-ears; and the remaining space, crowded with white pansies, silver-leaved white iris, and voluptuous white peonies. Whispering over all would be a silver willow-leaved pear tree.

No area is too small for planting. When space is limited, the wonders of container gardening can always be called upon: pots of feathery astilbe, nicotiana, agapanthus, or ranunculus grouped on an old wooden wheelbarrow, an étagère, a potting bench, or a ladder, in wooden crates, mossy garden baskets, or set in a row. In her *Garden Book,* Sackville-West wondered why "people don't use pot-plants more frequently . . . especially those people who have not a large garden and want to make use of every yard of space, easy to set a pot down on, taking up little room and giving little trouble apart from watering when the pots threaten to dry."

Our outdoor settings become compass points, the places where we gather our friends to share a light lunch on a peerless day; where we will go at night to breathe under the stars, as if in the center of a glorious bouquet; the places we hurry back to when we have been away.

A sunny porch is transformed into a sheltered escape, a getaway island, by a hammock made for drowsing. To add to the aura of delicious idleness: an ample straw hat to shade the eyes, a neck roll filled with rice hulls, an open book, and fresh fruit to nibble.

Open invitation: A white garden gate beckons
guests to a wooden kitchen table and folding café chairs
set up just beyond the house in the garden.
Above, ranunculus fill a small flower box enclosed in
looping iron wire, left, and a cachepot that resembles
the well-loved white picket fence, right.

*A longtime garden favorite
is the cast-iron settee.
The development of the metal
used for such extravagantly
whimsical furniture also
made possible the construction
of the great conservatories
and winter gardens, as
well as the skyscrapers of
the turn of the century.*

Spirits in White

The comfort of angels, robed in shimmering white, their great sheltering wings extended over us as we sleep, is a caressing tale from childhood, as consoling as the lullabies sung by a parent or grandparent. Perhaps it is this dream of being watched over by a tender guardian that keeps our hope of spirits alive. Indeed, winged goddesses and attendant sprites, muses, shamans, nymphs, and fairy folk, as well as archangels, seraphim, and cherubim have all caused the artistic imagination to take flight throughout history. The proof is everywhere: in the Winged Victory of Samothrace in the Louvre; Fra Angelico's musical angels on museum walls; the smiling seraph by the cathedral door at Reims. "In the mid-nineteenth century," writes art critic Herbert Muschamp, "a new breed of angel, neither Christian nor pagan, alights in the parks

Sprites, muses, and mothering goddesses, clockwise from top left: a fireplace keystone; a marble bust from the Vanderbilt estate in Shelbourne, Vermont; a plaque of the goddess Nike by Bertold Thorwaldsen.

and on the skylines of the Western world. . . . Allegorical figures of the virtues, of the arts, of peace, and of death, they hold olive branches, laurel wreaths, figures of the wounded, or fold their wings over statesmen and artists." These figures move lightly on top of columns, over fountains ~ heedless of wetting their feet ~ leaning, whispering, hurrying, almost always in motion. "Angels were a popular motif on nineteenth-century buildings," says restorer Michael Kempster of The Weeping Cherub, Essex, New York. His work brings him into constant contact with the angelic host, repairing now a broken wing, now a raised finger, now a lovely face. The descendant of four hundred years of master craftsmen, Michael not only refurbishes these endangered spirits by copying them in plaster casts, he brings them down to earth for admirers to take into their own homes.

Photography Credits